A 100 Yards from Utopia

A Collection of
Poems
and
Aphorisms

*

Ibrahim Ibn Salma

ASK Publishing
Santa Barbara, California
USA

ISBN: 978-0-9850376-3-5

First Edition
10 9 8 7 6 5 4 3 2 1

Cover & Book Design by Cesar Stanley Hernandez
Book Production by ASK Publishing

Photograph by Ana Ruth Flores

Published by ASK Publishing
1061 N. Patterson Ave
Santa Barbara, CA   93111
805-252-1207
askpublishing1@gmail.com

Other books by the author:

Traveler

A Poetic Odyssey by
Ibrahim Ibn Salma

Traveler: a collection of poems,   2012

A poetic odyssey, exploring the meaning of our spiritual nature. Through love and compassion we may gain more understanding of ourselves and the world around us. And, in the process, we may solidify our genuine and honest connection with family members, nature, our outer and inner worlds and the Divine. It is a journey of learning and discovery.

"Poets make the experience of life magical. The words of Traveler can move you into magic as reality"

> *William Edelen, Columnist*
> *The Santa Barbara News -press*

House of Love: a collection of poems,   2013

The poems of this collection are stepping stones. We step upon them to lead us to the House of Love. In the House of Love, love becomes our sole motivator. Once we enter, we shall never want to leave.

"The brutality of the world is taught in these pages how to move through mindfulness toward peace by ingenious verbal strategies that capture the complexity and ultimate healing simplicity of the power of love."

Barry Spacks, Poet-Professor, The First Poet laureate of the city of Santa Barbara, California

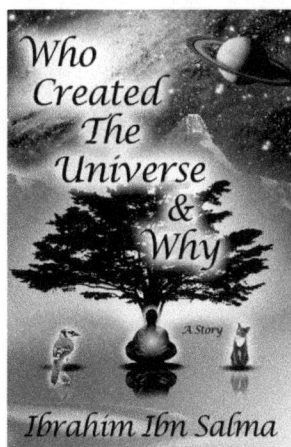

Who Created the Universe and Why: a spiritual parable with a poetic flavor. 2014

This story has the courage to explore a different way of thinking of what may have happened before the big bang which led to the manifestation of this wondrous universe.

"Paradise is not a different world; it is a different way to look at our world."

John Moriarty, Irish philosopher

Table of Contents

This collection addresses how
we compassionately act and react
toward ourselves and the world around us.

A 100 Yards from Utopia

I search for Utopia in
A dystopian world,
I descend valleys,
And ascend mountains,

I ask the wise
And not so wise,
I look for gold
And find dross,

I fret and fume
Swimming against the current -
Fatiguing myself in vain,

I repose,
A deep inhalation I take;

Utopia is
A hundred yards away,
If I only **Love**.

Birth

A drift in an antique kitchen,
A trembling between the legs,
Poignant, with no prior notice,

An eager feather, ready to fly off,
Head cocked, palpitating,
Impatient for an earthly existence,

Swimming out of the sanctuary
As a flamed bright fish,

With smooth painless dance,
And a cry of euphoria in utopia,

Surpassing the silence,
Echoed across the mountain of light.

"Nature humbles us with its magnificence."
Ibrahim Ibn Salma

Humility

I write, I am a writer,
A poem perhaps,
I am a poet.

The blackness of nights humbles me,
The full moon with its silver pen
Spells me –
I am written.

"What I kept I lost, what I spent I had, what I gave I have"
Persian proverb

Reaching

Uncover your body,
Naked,
The body of all bodies.

Open the blinds of your soul,
Strip off the bodies of your body,

Be vulnerable,

*

I will touch you with my Inner-Divine.

Broken Wings

I watch her,
Broken winged -
Singing melodies across
The night-day bridge -
Euphoric for a new day,
Joyous for the sun
To rise.

Undisturbed,
Unshaken,
By her calamity.

Her songs
Fill the air with tunes,
Soothing my ears,
Lifting my spirit,

Dumbfounded.

Re-Union

A wound that almost became a memory -
Is healed,
A vacuum of connection that haunted the hearts -
Is filled,

Our innocence
Taught us to wait,
What was in the hearts
Remains in the hearts,

A spark of a reminder
Of the love that
Has always been there;
A bond that was never shattered,
Never broken,
Never died.

*

The sun sets with its
Fire of passion,
The moon cools the heavens with its
Silver rays

And,
The rite of spring
Blooms with its roses,

Together,
They celebrate
Our re-union.

Aphorisms 01

'Poetry may sometimes yield to wisdom"
Ibrahim Ibn Salma

Death does not exist,
For there is no ending to who we are.

Self-trust is: knowing when you are
Powerful and when you are not.

Do not rid yourself of what you do not want,
Just focus on what you want.

This world is a solid thought, Death breaks it.

Love reduces the ripples in
A turbulent pond.

When the day undresses
The night of its darkness, I rise.

Loving words eliminate your enemies;
Your enemies become your friends.

The present is death to the past and
Birth to the future.

"Greed ultimately disperses the accumulated."
Arabic proverb, Translated by Ibrahim Ibn Salma

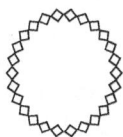

Greed kills the seed, Be munificent.

Ask for everything. Accept what is given.
Insist on none.

It is wiser not to look for yourself outside yourself.

Each rung of the life's ladder
Is a lesson we must learn in order to climb it.

Don't be concerned of what you do not know.
Be concerned of what you know for sure to be true
But in fact it is not true.

Sizes

How big would I like to be?
Big enough to embrace the universe
Within me.

How tall would I like to be?
Tall enough to reach my full potential.

How short would I like to be?
Short enough to walk in your shadow.

How small would I like to be?
Small enough to fit with you
In tiny places.

Self-Growth

He who speaks
Of good deeds
Knocks on the door

*

He who does
Good deeds
Finds the door open.

Similitude;

Do ordinary tasks
You knock on the door,

*

Do extraordinary tasks
You find the door open.

Self-Empowerment

A teacher is
A Student;

To teach others is
Self-teaching,

To empower others is
Self-empowerment.

California Drought

Enough now of no rain,
Enough now of dry eyes of winter,
Day by day, green is fading,
Women returning with
Empty baskets of roses,

I take it all in,
I wait, I pray for,
The waterfall to fall again, for
The lakes to be
Full again, for
The creeks to
Flow again,

I take it all in,
I wait, I pray, for
The droplets
To return home.

Hard Times

California drought 2014

Hence a full claret cup,
Too dry for my sport,
The wine over brimmed
All summer long,
I drink enough of
Golden sunshine
Till my brain feels
The dry-lake pain,

There is a beverage,
Healthier and brighter,
The cup is the sky.

To the gods of
The east and the west
My soul has flown
Above my head
With a merciful fist,
To fill the mother's breasts
For the thirsty child,
To look afar at
The green of the hill,

To drink from
An endless fountain
Pouring upon me from
The heaven's brook.

Aphorisms 02

Simplicity is the beginning of knowledge.

Where there is a rose, there is a thorn.
It is up to us which one to pick.

Reason makes believe
What faith cannot.

I am a gladiator in the arena of reason
And persuasion and not of depredation.

The longer my body lives
The more it dies.

Being alone gives me
The ineffable luxury of owning my time.

He who masters others
Allows himself to be mastered.

Life's garden blisters with weeds,
But we can always weed our garden.

When we read and learn
We hurt no one.

Liberty relies on the inner well-being.

Patience is a holy writ.

Self-love is to claim what's yours.
Selfishness is to claim someone else's.

To be free is to accept your limitations.

If freedom is not given to you,
No one can take away from you.

Love is the only spider
That does not make cobwebs.

Love in the heart
Immunizes it from heart attacks.

An ounce of love weighs more
Than a ton of hate.

When you work for life,
Life would work for you.

Be the moon in someone's dark life.

Accepting our differences
Is the first step to know one another.

Accept a defeat,
But do not be defeated.

Always have a thoughtful action
To establish order.

We may not know who and what we are,
But we always have the opportunity to find out.

Give thy thoughts to thy hearts.

Ode to Gaza Strip

Your strip is no longer a strip.
Like a stranger who is not
Sure of the street or the house,
Something takes life away
In the depths of what are ashes.
Glass trembles with every explosion
Which falls and sets it on fire.

A vast cry goes out to the islands,
Through a wounded doorway to the sea,
Marked with your ruptured scarlet veins,
Which falls on a deaf ear.

You want to restore living in dignity -
Brutally rejected.

Sometimes when you stop being,
Stop coming and stop going
Under blankets of ruins
And the heavy feet of death;
Rise, my dear, rise
Like stepped on dust,
Maya's dust.

Restore Love

Parisian Massacre

Death loomed, destruction mounted,
God was replaced with human cruelty,

The click of a dystopian ideology;
Fracturing the innocence,
And the neon lights,
The city of light rendered dark,
Walking upon the ruins of the future,
The Eiffel Tower wept;
Red, white and blue
Drops of grief,

They peeled off blood, they killed,
We shed blood, we killed, we droned,
And returned to bomb the rubble and the corpses,
When will it all end?

Insane men they are,
Sane and free men we think we are,
Can we not stop this vicious cycle of death?
I wonder,

Oh trouble, be kind,
I have no taste for vengeance,
Our democracy is emptied of meaning.

Journey

Written for Ferguson and New York

Dreams caressing the eyes
Of the awakened,
Sailing upon the crests
Of imagination,
Breaking off the past
From the future,
Celebrating the present.

Plenty of opportunities
To establish order,
A self-governing -
Not in fears and follies of man –
But in reason and persuasion,

Founded on benevolence,
With more pleasure than pain,

Leaving fear astern;
Where we do not shoot,
We are able to breathe,
And
Black lives matter.

War

Written to celebrate the signing
Of the Iran nuclear agreement

A crimson affliction, where
Chaos and destructions are
As real and vibrant as reason,
Innocence is the main casualty,
Earthquake shocking
The landscape of conviction,
A world unable to cope
With catastrophe and carnage,
Glory, honor and courage are
Hollow and empty alongside
The lifeless corpses and
The scarlet rivers,
Smokes rise from the ruins,
Screaming to
The soul of humanity their pains,
Echoing over the valleys and
The mountains to halt
The killings, the destructions,
The decimations.
The voice of reason is heard
When the Iran
Nuclear agreement is signed.

War of Colors

Upon yellow sand of a distant land,
There existed a kingdom, 'The **Yellow** Kingdom',
The people and their clothes were **Yellow**,
Yellow were the houses, the streets and the trees,
The animals of all kinds were also **Yellow**,
The **Yellow** laws governed the land and the people.

Then there was a moment of shock and awe:
The **Yellow** kingdom discovered the existence
Of a **Blue** Kingdom,
Where people and things were **Blue**.
And the Yellow kingdom decided the Blue kingdom
Posed a threat to the **Yellow** freedom and democracy.
They also possessed Weapons of Mass destruction,
Of the **Blue** kind,
And they must change to **Yellow** or die.

Armed with buckets of **Yellow** paint,
The **Yellow** kingdom deployed their troops
Ready to attack, to defend itself,
The **Blue** Kingdom filled their buckets
With **Blue** paint,
The **Yellow** army was pouring **Yellow** paint
Over the **Blue** army to change its color,
The **Blue** army was showering the **Yellow**
Army with **Blue** paint.

Two weeks of fighting elapsed
And the two armies suddenly
Stopped the fight,
Looked at each other in shock.
No more **Yellow** and **Blue** but one color,
Green.

Emptiness

A once chanting love renders silent,
A crow aimlessly flies in despair,
Hungry,
Unfulfilled.
A blue jay with blue-less wings,
Rain without raindrops,
Rainbow in a colorless state.

A loveless heart,
In an empty tiger,
Helot.

Gratitude-s

Thank you for the good health.

Thank you moon for
Reflecting the beauty of the sunlight
So that I am able to look at it.

Thank you sun for welcoming me every
Morning when I am reborn from
The womb of sleep.

Thank you legs for walking a step ahead
Of me so that I won't fall.

Thank you dark night,
For letting me see the stars.

Thank you chair,
For being the tool I use to sit above the ground.

Thank you dust,
For reminding us of our bodies' roots.

Thank you muscles for helping me
Walk the extra mile.

Patience

To insist on actions and
Never be still,
Is not the way of the mountain,

Things never have a purpose
When they are chased;

The wise poet
Waits for the poem to peep,

The wise hunter
Never exercises his will,

The wise woman
Speaks when
Her soul moves,

The baby bird
Never soars until
She is ready to fly.

Patience loves to
Hug a tree and relax
On her trunk.

Have no Clue

There is something inside her attracts me
I have no clue what it is,

There is a sensation that draws me close to her
I have no clue what it is.

I can see it through her beautiful smile,
I can sense it coming from the depth of her eyes,
And I have no clue what it is

I can hear it when she recites,
I can pay close attention when she speaks
Her peaceful voice rings with her loving words
And I still have no clue what it is,

She once told me she left her heart in Africa.
Can I bring it back to America?
I have no clue.

We watch the sunsets together.
We gaze at the stars and the heavens.
We hike with one another.

Where will the sunsets lead me to?
What will the stars reveal to me?
Where will the hikes guide me to?
I have no clue.

Revelation

Come closer dear one, said the voice:
I am the thing inside her that attracts you.
I am the clue.

I am the sensation that draws you close to her.
I am the clue.

I smile through her beautiful face.
I see with her deep eyes.
And I am the clue.

My words are what she recites.
Loving as they sound when
Her peaceful voice rings deep inside.
And I am the clue.

I am the Mother.
I am the children.
I am the drawings she draws.
I am her poetry, and I am her prose.

I am the sunsets which she watches.
I am the stars at which she gazes.
I am the trails on which she hikes.
And I am the clue.

She is my embodiment.
She is the feet I walk on.
And she is the heart I love with.

And above all, she is my body and
I am her soul.
But I am still the clue that
Will stay forever with you.

One

Amid feathers of silk,
Two souls are wrapped,
Gently they merge,
One they become.

Separated

I am not black,
But,
The night with its
Wings
Blackened me.

The cavaliers on
Their horses
Passed me by.

They left me behind,
Took my beloved
Away from me.

I am separated.

Forget

They say forget her,
I say;
Show me a heart of stone
That can forget,

In my memory
Of loving her
I have strengthened
My longing for love,

I have tasted
The beauty of clasping
When my arms danced
Around her,

Our spoken words ceased
When our eyes met,

The stars of the dark sky
Dazzled like diamonds
When our lips touched,

Our bodies waltzed
Above the horizon
When we made love,

Would you forget?

Yes

Yes is a three letter word.
The 'Y' is to Yield to your reality.
The 'E' is to Elevate above mediocrity.
The 'S' is to Surrender to your spirituality.

*

So my friend, say always YES
And never criticize.
Peace and harmony
In your life
Will surely be realized.

I Pray

I pray that humans solve their differences
Without having to fight one another.

I pray that humans can live together in harmony
Despite their dissension.

I pray that humans realize that
Initiating harm to another
Will ultimately cause harm to the initiator.
For we will reap hate when we cultivate hate.

I pray that we all sow love
So that more love would grow.

I pray, I pray, and I pray.

Unrealized Self

Dimly known,
Almost untouched,
Nearly untapped,
Causing a conflict between
The 'yes' and the 'no',
Emotional responses
To the foggy and misty aspects of life,
A world without essence,
Relying on the outsides for comfort,
Creating the uneasiness within.

*

The un-fulfilled hope for a better future
Is overlooked;
Where nature is from the inside;
The simplicity of the self,
The imaginative part of the soul
To manifest the un-manifested;
The greater part of one's existence,
For more completeness and unity
To establish a sense of joy to
The real self.

Harmony

Front cover

In a field of hyacinths,
Glimmering her black beauty,
A composer of euphonic melodies,
Caressing the ivory and ebony keys,
Chanting the harmony of existence;

In a world,
Where the large and the small,
The giant and not so giant,
The rich and not so rich;
The strong and the weak

Can share the fragrance of
A peaceful life.

Aphorisms 03

Everything ever exists
Is a product of thought.

Faith precludes
Intellectual and critical thinking.

Write your own unique poem
Before you drop your body.

Be naught what you do,
Do what you are.

Not knowing what to do
May lead you to a true knowing.

O' life I had borrowed you from light
And to light I shall deliver you.

Give a space to others
Without losing yours.

Lose yourself before you profoundly find it.

57

When the objectivity of reality meets
The subjectivity of consciousness,
We may begin to unlock
The mystery of creation.

Non-violence is one way to overcome bullies
Without being a thug.

Real power is the ability
To empower others.

Tragedies can sometimes be blessings.

A dead fish will always go with the flow,
Don't be a dead fish.

Be aware of the miracle
Of getting an eyeful of the stars.

Are you tired of hearing about racism?
Imagine for a moment
How tiring it is
To suffer because of it.

Nature humbles us with its magnificence.

Be an anvil to support rather than
A hammer to strike.

One mouth, two ears,
Shouldn't we listen more?

Revolutions are never crumbs,
They are sparked by crumbs.

An abused child needs
Naught to be an abusive parent.

Do not wait for the storm to pass,
Learn how to go through it.

To truly survive is to be most loving.

If an opportunity knocks on your door,
Open the door and let it in.

Spending one's life seeking light,
Avoiding dark and its beauty;
Stars are only seen in its presence.

Make yourself happy before
You make others happy.

Do not chase after your dreams,
Allow them to manifest themselves.

To fully be free is
To allow others to be free.

The most generous is
The most virtuous.

Honesty is
A scimitar of brutality to one's self,
A gift of diplomacy to another.

Always have the things you prefer in life,
But do not let them control you.

Hatred is never diminished by more hatred,
It is however reduced by love.

Wear away injustice,
Like water wearing away stones.

Consciousness + Thought = Spiritual Being,
Spiritual Being + Physical Body = Physical Being,
Physical Being + Spiritual Being = Full being.

Ultimately there exits only one law;
There are no laws.

The small is as big as the large,
When there are no boundaries.

Do not be excessive in anything,
Even virtue.

How is it they live in such harmony,
The trillions cells in our bodies?

Self-compassion gives you the ability
To have compassion for others.

Speeches of a few words with great meanings
Are the most profound.

A rigid heart touched by love –
Softens.

Denude

Denude Machiavelli, "The ends justify the means."

Regard not the ends,
Focus on the means,
The ends will follow.

Glowing

Star to star,
How distant,
Dark matter hinders,
Yet;
Stars keep glowing through.

Dentist

Written for my dentist
Dr. Peppard

Gracefully navigating,
Detoxifying the landscape,
Removing the impurities,
Extracting the afflicted.

In-laying the foundation
For a bright future,
Building bridges
For safety,
Drilling holes,
Filling fissures with ore.

Implanting peace subcutaneously,
Rooting canals
To feed the glutton.

Whitening the tools -
A smile to life in perpetuity.

A true healer,
An angel in disguise
A dentist.

Ode to Socks

Celebrating your pairings,
Twinning in joy,
A green-house enclave
Of lower extremities,
With a soft landing on earth,
Keeping away
The anomaly of the environment,
As roses, you pride yourselves
With your colorful existence,
A threesome pleasure
When the night falls,
You patiently await,
Sleeping, perhaps
Not in tranquility,
You eagerly want to
Slide and slide
To brighten the world
Where you perfectly fit.

I Create

I choose, therefore I create.
I decide, therefore I create.
I think, therefore I create.
I feel, therefore I create.
I believe, therefore I create.
I ask my Goddess's assistance
Therefore I co-create.

*

My reality is a product of
My attitudes, my desires
And my imagination.

Poet's Craze

They float about my mind,
I can't help but rhyme,
I do it all the time.

I even charge a nickel per line,
But today I settle for a dime.

I recite all the hours,
About these crazy flowers.

I squeak when I speak.

Sometimes they do not make sense,
Even if I jump over the fence.

Now I relax on my cute ass,
And light a joint of grass.

Aphorisms 04

Stillness is a spiritual growth made visible.

Let your deepest-self
Reveal it-self to you.

Mix your giving with
A brief moment of receptivity.

Gratitude is authentic when you allow
The experience to spiritually elevate you.

God is about love and compassion
Not enforcement and compulsion.

Nature is our ocean.

Water in a bottle
Becomes the bottle --
Be like water.

I am loved for who I am,
Therefore I am joyous.

You hold all the playing cards of the deck,
Do not give any card away.

He who is afraid of death,
Is afraid of life.

We always make choices in life,
Choices do not make us.

Be not concerned more
With the pursuit of happiness than
The happiness of pursuit.

Searching for a solution
Is wiser than avoiding the problem.

Quest for a glimpse of light
Through the cracks of life.

Real happiness is in surrendering and dreaming,
Not in resisting and laboring.

I searched for God,
I found Love.

I am afraid of height,
But when you lift me higher I am safe.

Glide above a turbulent ocean
Instead of swimming against the current.

Real love does not
Demand love in return.

Impassioned love always enslaves the lovers
And ultimately leads to more pain than pleasure.

Khadija

Our merrymaking now ended;
She was an angel,
A piece of heaven
Melted into thin air,

The great palace,
The festive temple,
And the earth itself,
Which are inherited
Shall now dissolve -
Become mournful.

Her siblings, offspring and
Their offspring whose lives
Rendered hollow
Are solemn,

She is what
Sweet dreams are made of,
A rose that never wilts,
A light that shines forever.

God bless your soul
Sister Khadija.

The most beloved name
To the prophet Mohammed.

A Smiling Face

A tribute to the Mona-Lisa

A mystery beneath the eyeful face,
Hiding, shying away from a violent world,
A smile that makes
The moon blush,
A true euphoric luxury
In a sad world,
Offering tranquility and serenity.

Beauty hidden beneath all beauties,

*

I ask;
Would the face reveal
Its hidden treasure?
I wonder!

Would the smile
Expose its poetic nature?
I ponder!

Yet,
The smile and the face will
Employ the eyes of humanity
Forever.

Aphorisms 05

When you become a member of an ideology,
You lose your capacity to be unique.

Spirituality is not a mystical world elsewhere,
It is a valuable part of this life that
Stems from being alive.

Patriotism is a cult.

If compassion is the flute, love is the breath.

Create moments of lasting consequences.

A poet is a secular priest.

Heavens and hells are more states of mind
Than particular and real places.

Reacting while angry is
Worse than sailing through a storm.

You have unlimited power when
You control your anger.

When you judge you are bound,
When you accept you are free.

Compassion is the scent of the wise.

A good word always touches the heart.

Always learn, even from your enemy.

The tongue of the wise is always behind his heart,
The heart of the unwise is behind his tongue.

"Harm shall not be inflicted,
Nor shall it be reciprocated."
Prophet Mohamed (PBUP)

Do not authenticate the praise of
A person who does not know you.

Be friending a heart
Who values solitude.

Water is for the trees to grow,
Tears are for the cheeks to glow.

If you try to falsify the facts you lose.

Travel the road of your life with a smile
Rather than with a gun.

Do not put yourself
In a position of incrimination,
You have yourself to blame.
P. Mohamed (PBUH)

"You talk about God a lot, and you make me feel guilty
by using that word. You better watch out!
That word will poison you, if you use it
to have power over me."

Rumi

Sacred Secret

I once visited my house of worship,
God holding a chalice of wine,
Intoxicated,
A sacred secret slurred:

"Nothing to forgive,
Nothing to judge,
Nothing to feel guilty about
Because
There is no sin."

Oh my!
How wisely
Intoxicating.

All the Love

All the love I can embody
Is dedicated to you.

All the lives I choose to live,
I live for you.

Oh - my beloved,
My existence
Belongs to you.

I drink from
Your endless river
Of compassion -
When thirsty.

I eat from
Your garden
Of passion -
When hungry.

My heart beats
In harmony
With your songs.

My soul vibrates
In resonance
With your souls

Oh Goddess and God
I am so joyous
To have known you.

Aphorisms 06

Take care of the flower,
For it will give you the fruit.

Love is learning to tolerate
The intolerable.

Whatever is said might be an art,
But silence is a very fine art.

Compassion is to **com**bine ourselves and
The world around us with **passion.**

Be true to your teeth,
They will otherwise be false to you.

Let the stem grow into a rose.

Look for the loaf of bread within
Rather than the crumbs without.

Drop and release what is not
Love within you.

Travel the road within
Rather than the road without.

He who fears nothing
Loves everything.

Let love infuse
Your emotions.

"Do **unto others** as you would have them
do **unto you.**"
Jesus Christ

"Fight in the way of God
Those who fight you,
But do not begin hostilities,
For God does not like the aggressor."
Quran (2:190)

A thoughtful person is sensitive enough
To hear the unspoken words.

We are entities of consciousness,
Always seeking to know more of ourselves.

Life is sweet if I accept its bitterness.

93

Imagination is the sole provision
Of a spiritual traveler.

There never exists a tree
Whose branches kill one another.

Deep inside us we are the same.

To have is to die a little everyday,
To be is never to cease being born.

94

"*Ancora Imparo*"

I

  am

    Still

      Learning

        Michelangelo

*

"*Paradise is not a different world; it is a different way to look at our world.*"

John Moriarty, Irish philosopher

With Peace & Love.

Ibrahim Ibn Salma

Acknowledgments

I am very grateful to my friend Michael Hegewald for suggesting the title of this book. I am also grateful to Mahdy Khaiyat for inspiring me to continue writing and to my friends Eleanor Grandfield and Birgitta Hansson, for closely following and editing my work. I also thank Ana Ruth Flores and Cesar Stanley Hernandez for their artistic talents.

Rumi's quotes are translated by Coleman Barks.

Ibrahim is a poet and a spiritual scientist.
He has been inspired by nature and her soul,
by a world whose purpose of existence
is to be most loving and by his affinity
with his growth as a spiritual being, which
he takes very seriously. He has been writing
poems and aphorisms reflecting his intention
to grow spiritually.

Printed in
The United States of America